Consultants

Ashley Bishop, Ed.D.

Sue Bishop, M.ED.

Publishing Credits

Dona Herweck Rice, *Editor-in-Chief*

Robin Erickson, *Production Director*

Lee Aucoin, *Creative Director*

Sharon Coan, *Project Manager*

Jamey Acosta, *Editor*

Rachelle Cracchiolo, M.A.Ed., *Publisher*

Image Credits

cover Romanchuck Dimitry/Shutterstock; p.2 Romanchuck Dimitry/Shutterstock; p.3 thumb/Shutterstock; p.4 Imageman/Shutterstock; p.5 Jim Barber/Shutterstock; p.6 ericlefrancais/Shutterstock; p.7 Katrina Brown/Shutterstock; p.8 Bragin Alexey/Shutterstock; p.9 Ultrashock/Shutterstock; p.10 vseb/Shutterstock; back cover Bragin Alexey/Shutterstock

Teacher Created Materials

5301 Oceanus Drive
Huntington Beach, CA 92649-1030
http://www.tcmpub.com

ISBN 978-1-4333-2565-6
© 2012 Teacher Created Materials, Inc.
Printed in China
Nordica.072018.CA21800635

I like the **o**ctopus.

I like the box.

I like the socks.

I like the clock.

I like the pot.

I like the mop.

I like the rock.

I like the fox.

I like the log.

Glossary

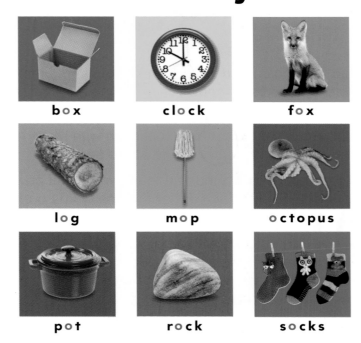

box

clock

fox

log

mop

octopus

pot

rock

socks

Sight Words

I   like   the

Activities

- Read the book aloud to your child, pointing to the short *o* words as you say them. After reading each page, ask, "What do you like?"

- Have your child start a rock collection with rocks he or she finds around your home or at the park.

- Go to a park with a pond and teach your child how to skip rocks. Remind him or her that the words *pond* and *rocks* have the short *o* sound.

- Make a yarn octopus with a ball of yarn and some wobbly eyes from a craft store. For more detailed directions, you can search on the Internet for "how to make a yarn octopus."

- Help your child think of a personally valuable word to represent the short *o* sound, such as *mom*.